For Harry

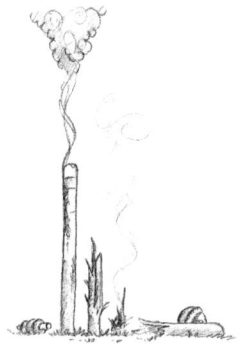

The Ashes Illustrated

A COLLECTION OF PENCIL
CARTOONS & CARICATURES
DETAILING THE ASHES SERIES
OF 2019

EDGBASTON | LORD'S | HEADINGLEY | OLD TRAFFORD | THE OVAL

First Published 2019

Copyright Patrick Latham 2019

A Print on Demand Book
by Amazon

ISBN: 9781694465085

Typesetting and Origination by Patrick Latham
Printed in GB by Amazon

www.aleadingedge.co.uk

Follow on social media for up to date news #aleadingedge

Contents

Tim Paine's Ashes Speech

We shall go on to the end, mate!

We shall fight in England;

We shall fight at Edgbaston, and Lord's.

We shall fight, with growing confidence
   and growing strength at the crease.

We shall defend our totals, mate,
   whatever the cost may be.

Look.. We shall fight in the outfields,

We shall fight on every cricket ground.

We shall fight with the bat and the ball,

We shall fight at the Oval,

We shall never surrender, mate!

A Warm (and slightly damp) Welcome to Edgbaston!

The scoreboard operators at Edgbaston cunningly left the scoreboard showing the final score of the World Cup semi final match between England and Australia as a nice welcome for the Australians...

Rain gets in the way of preparations ahead of day one.

Welcome to Edgbaston Australia!

31st July 2019

Ben Stokes is reported as saying that we should 'expect theatre' in the 2019 Ashes Series..

1st Ashes Test Match

- Edgbaston -

Day 1

An amusing final few bars of the National Anthem relaxed the England players who went on to put Australia in trouble.

Think what you like of Steve Smith, the booing was unnecessary, the guy is a magician with the bat. Along with Peter Siddle and Nathan Lyon, he got the Aussies right out of jail with a magnificent 100. Great to see Stuart Broad with 5 wickets!

Hoping England can bat all day tomorrow and on into Saturday!

Close: Australia 284/ao (Smith 144, Broad 5/86)

Day 2

What a day for Rory Burns!

Not often two boys from the same school head out to open the batting in an Ashes Test for England! He might not have the most traditional set up, but it seems to work for him.

A change of ball brought an end to English fortunes as the 'new' older ball did something! Joe Root bottled some Irish luck from last week, but as England got up near the Australian first innings score with 6 wickets left it was definitely Rory's day, 125*!

Well batted!

Close: England 267/4 (Burns 125)*

Day 3

Another day of twists and turns with England recovering well to get well ahead of Australia on first innings. Great to see Stuart Broad spend time in the middle and help England to a lead.

Word of spectators being relieved of their sandpaper at the gates.. I can imagine it was fun for security to try to get some of the punters in line!

The Edgbaston crowd made themselves known on fancy dress Saturday. The Hollies stand were in great voice. The Steve Smith problem goes on for England..

The test could go either way in the next 2 days! Beautifully set up!

Close: England 374/ao (Burns 133), Australia 124/3

3rd August 2019

Day 4

The man is a machine.. incredible effort as SPD Smith scores yet another Ashes 100 allowing Australia to declare, setting England a huge task on the final day.

The 'Smith Wall' was eventually negotiated, but on a turning pitch with variable bounce on day 5, there is a really tough uphill journey ahead to firstly get past the loss, then the draw, and on to what would be a huge win!

Then on to Lord's.....

Close: Australia 487/7 dec (Smith 142), England 13/0

4th August 2019

Day 5

It was always going to be a tough ask, but thoughts of pressure on Nathan Lyon with the weight of expectation on him might have been enough to give England a chance..

The ball went sideways and up and down... all luck used up... as the wickets went down it was only a matter of time!

The GOAT, Nathan Lyon, bowled England out to put Australia 1-0 up as the teams get ready for Lord's next week.

Close: England 146/ao (Lyon 6/49)

England Lose by 251 runs

England 0 | Australia 1

5th August 2019

After the 1st Test, it is obvious that Steve Smith
is going to have a huge influence on this series..

"Someone make sure that 'S.M.U.D.G.E' thing
is fully recharged before Lord's!"

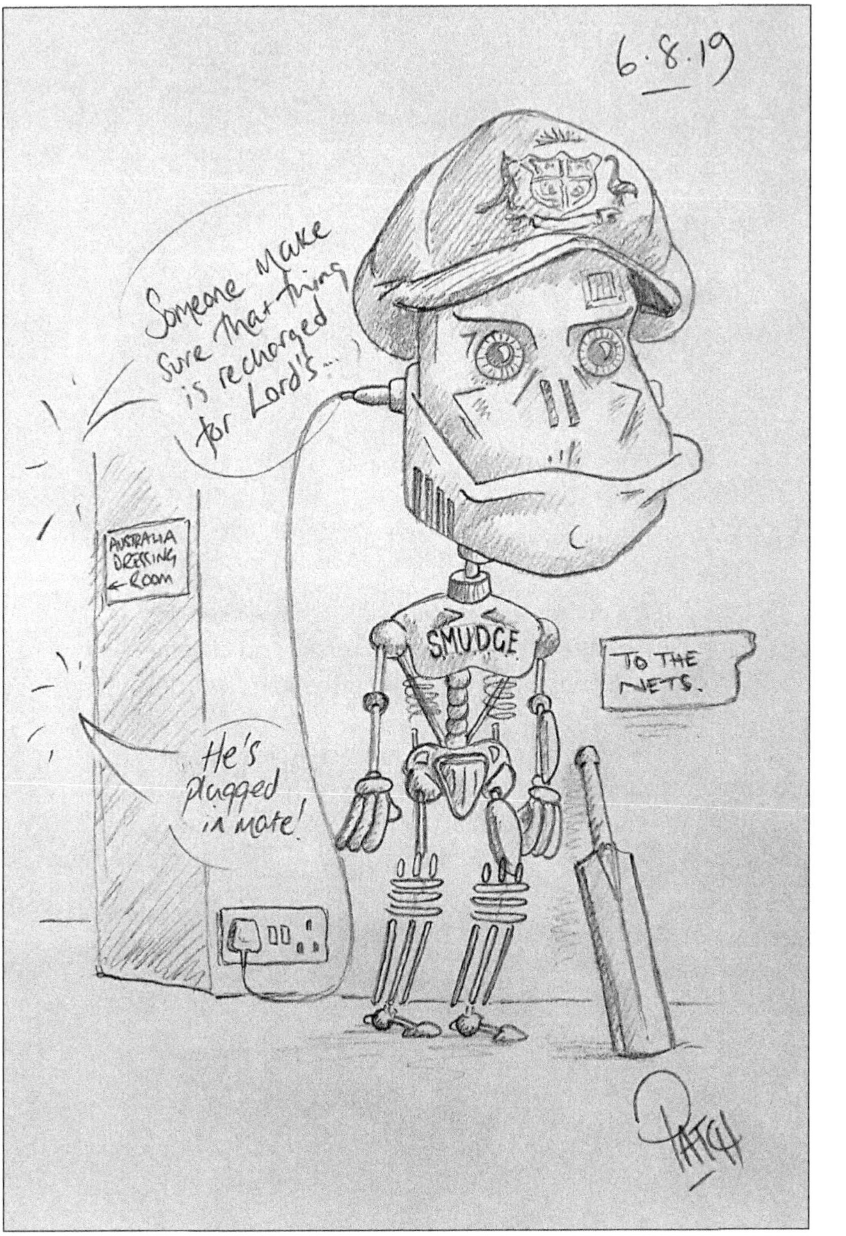

6th August 2019

Jofra Archer scores 100 and takes 6 wickets for Sussex against Gloucestershire in a 2nd XI game, proving he now is fit to play after injury worries.

It leaves some of the Gloucester players and trialists wondering if perhaps he had mistaken their county badge for a similar one from another team...

7th August 2019

Questions raised over who is
actually in charge out there...

"Directions from the Australian cordon..."

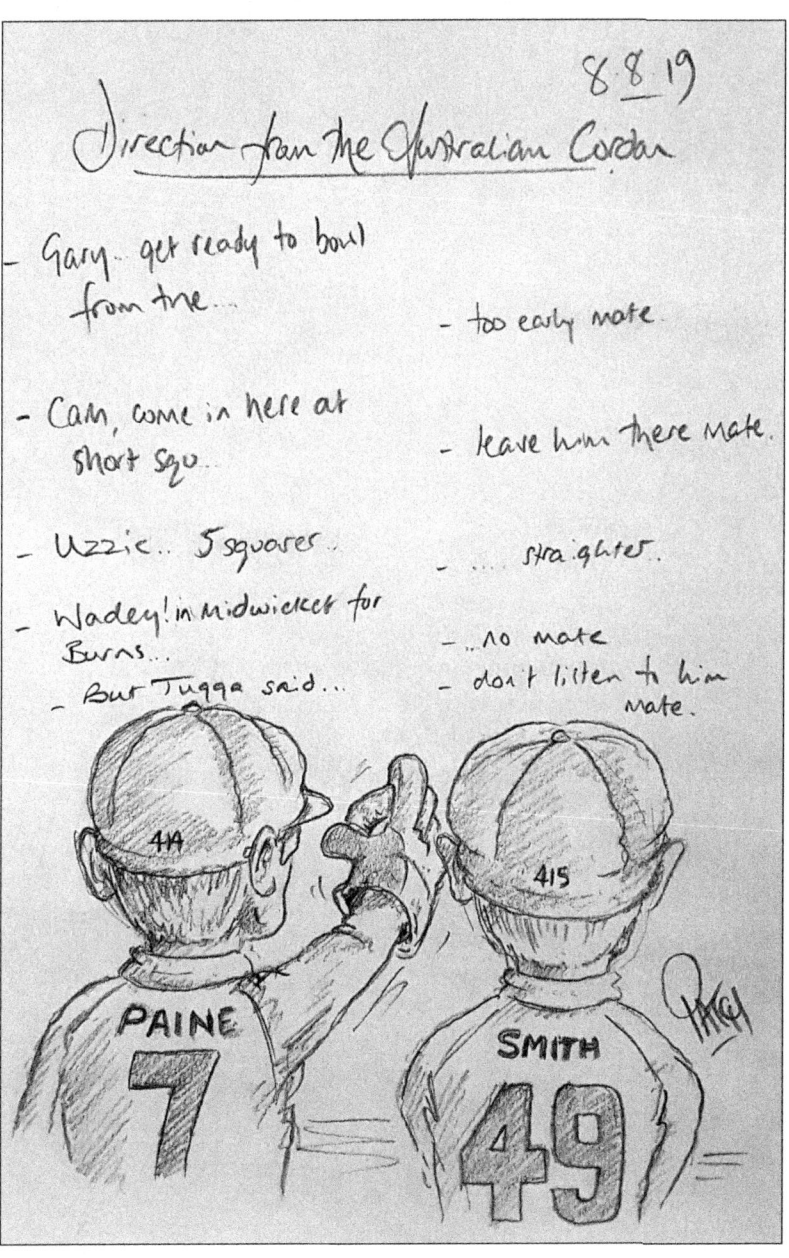

8th August 2019

With time running out to come up with ideas
on dealing with Steve Smith before the
2nd Test at Lord's, Trevor Bayliss enlists
the dubious assistance of some outside consultants...

9th August 2019

With Trevor's injury list growing and having seen the zorbing at Lord's last week on TV, he has come up with a way of protecting his players from further niggles ahead of the 2nd Test on Wednesday...

10th August 2019

This morning, the first MCC member arrived
to form the queue at the Grace Gates
a full 3 days before the first ball is bowled
in the Lord's Test match.

By 11am on Wednesday, he will be fast asleep
in the Library in his favourite arm chair
using a copy of The Times as a duvet
and will miss every single ball of the day...

The first MCC member arrives 11.8.19 at the Grace Gates a full 3 days before the 1st ball of the Lord's Test. By 11am on Wednesday he will be fast asleep in the Library under the newspaper...

11th August 2019

James Taylor takes his thoughts on team
selection to Ed Smith ahead of the Lord's Test...

12th August 2019

Ahead of the likely debut of Jofra Archer,
Justin Langer tries his hand at a bit of
pre match sledging only to have Jofra
close him down with ease...

2nd Ashes Test Match

Lord's

Day 1

It is always an incredible experience to be in the
Long Room at Lord's, but an extra bonus being
in here to be able to draw today's entry.

Frustrating to get so close to play only
for the rain to return..

Changing Room cricket is for all of us...
'Steady Jof... Save those ones for tomorrow!'

Rain all day..

14th August 2019

Day 2

It will be quite a remarkable day at Lord's today,
and whilst the cricket will be thrilling,
the overwhelming theme of the day will be
#RedForRuth and the @ruthstraussfoundation.

Good luck to the players, supporters and of course
the Strauss family.

Have a great day out!

Close: England 258/ao, Australia 30/1

www.ruthstraussfoundation.com

15th August 2019

Day 3

Another wet day at Lord's, with Captain Dar
and Able Seaman Gaffaney on another
search and rescue mission out to the middle
to try to locate the wicket...

Close: Australia 80/4

16th August 2019

Day 4

A fantastic day of Test Match cricket,
incredible head to head battle between
Jofra Archer and Steve Smith.

Sadly, a number of cricket 'fans'
continue to boo certain players.

Enough now we think folks!

Save the boos for your Christmas panto!

Close: Australia 250/ao (Smith 90), England 96/4

17th August 2019

Day 5

An incredible Ashes 2019 chapter comes to a close
in a hard fought draw at HQ.

In a day that saw a concussed Steve Smith
come out to bat in a Marnus Laubschagne
mask to score a match saving 50
during which he wore another horrific
ball of doom from Archer,
the Aussie kit man has started modifying
the batting gear for the 3rd Test up at Headingley...

Close: England 285/5 dec, Australia 154/6

Match Drawn

England 0 | Australia 1

With all the clanging of ball off helmet and body at Lord's,
even the Australian mascots were getting uneasy..

"The kangaroo was talking about learning to
walk backwards and then the emu got quite difficult....."

A subtle change to the Australian crest
pacify the kangaroo and the emu.

19·8·19

"The Kangaroo was talking about leaning
to walk backwards... Then the emu
joined in and was getting a bit difficult...

So we adjusted the logo and
gave them the protection they
were after."

PATCH

19th August 2019

"A Bouncer War.....?"

It's all go for Thursday at Headingley!

20th August 2019

Australian captain Tim Paine has called for the best version of David Warner in the absence of Steve Smith through the concussion injury suffered in the Lord's Test. After Dave's amazingly poor start to the series with the bat, it would be important he gets it right here...

"No.. Not what I meant, Dave..."

21st August 2019

3rd Ashes Test Match

-Headingley-

Day 1

A frustrating rain affected day seeing early
Resistance by Warner and co, but a late
flurry of Australian wickets leave England
on top at having bowled the Aussies out for 179.

Concerns about the continued overuse
of Jofra Archer as he takes six-fer!

Close: Australia 179/ao (Archer 6/45)

22nd August 2019

Day 2

How quickly this game can take to wind out of your sails...

From flying high yesterday after seeing off the Australians to being blown away by the superhero trio of Cummins, Pattinson and Hazlewood:

England are now in deep poop.

Close: England 67/ao (Hazlewood 5/30), Australia 171/6

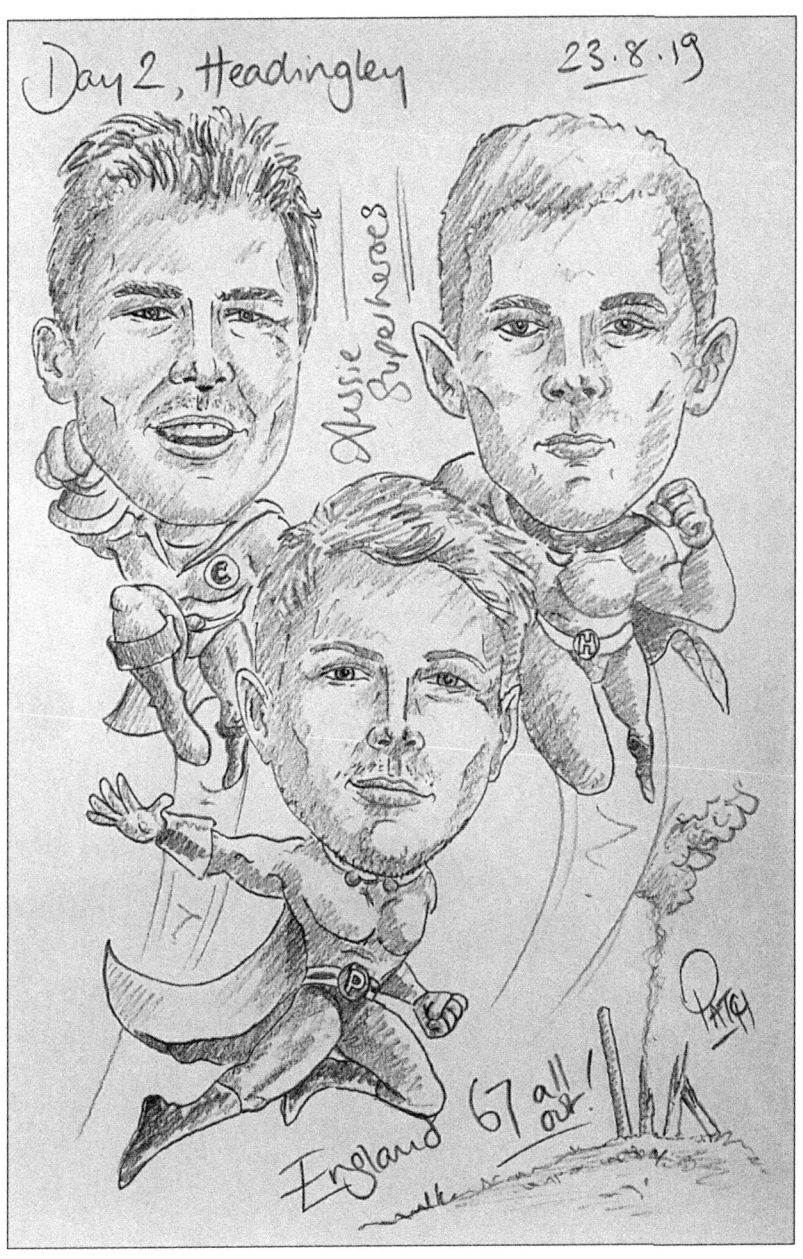

Day 3

More extraordinary brave resistance by the
annoyingly immovable, bubblegum blowing
Human punch ball concussion replacement
Marnus Laubschagne put Australia right out of reach…

Or are they…?

If England are only 4 down after lunch
tomorrow it could be a right nipper!

Close: Australia 246/ao (Laubschagne 80), England 156/3

Day 4

Can you believe it....? What an incredible day!

Ben Stokes and Jack Leach in a remarkably dramatic last gasp partnership to swing England back into the Ashes race!

Close: 362/9 (Stokes 135*, Leach 1*)

England win by one wicket.

England 1 | Australia 1

Meanwhile, in some leafy suburb
on the outskirts of Leeds..

"Dad... you know those 'Day 5' tickets
you got for the Headingley Test...?

Did you read the date..?"

26th August 2019

The types of delivery that are
making The Ashes 2019..

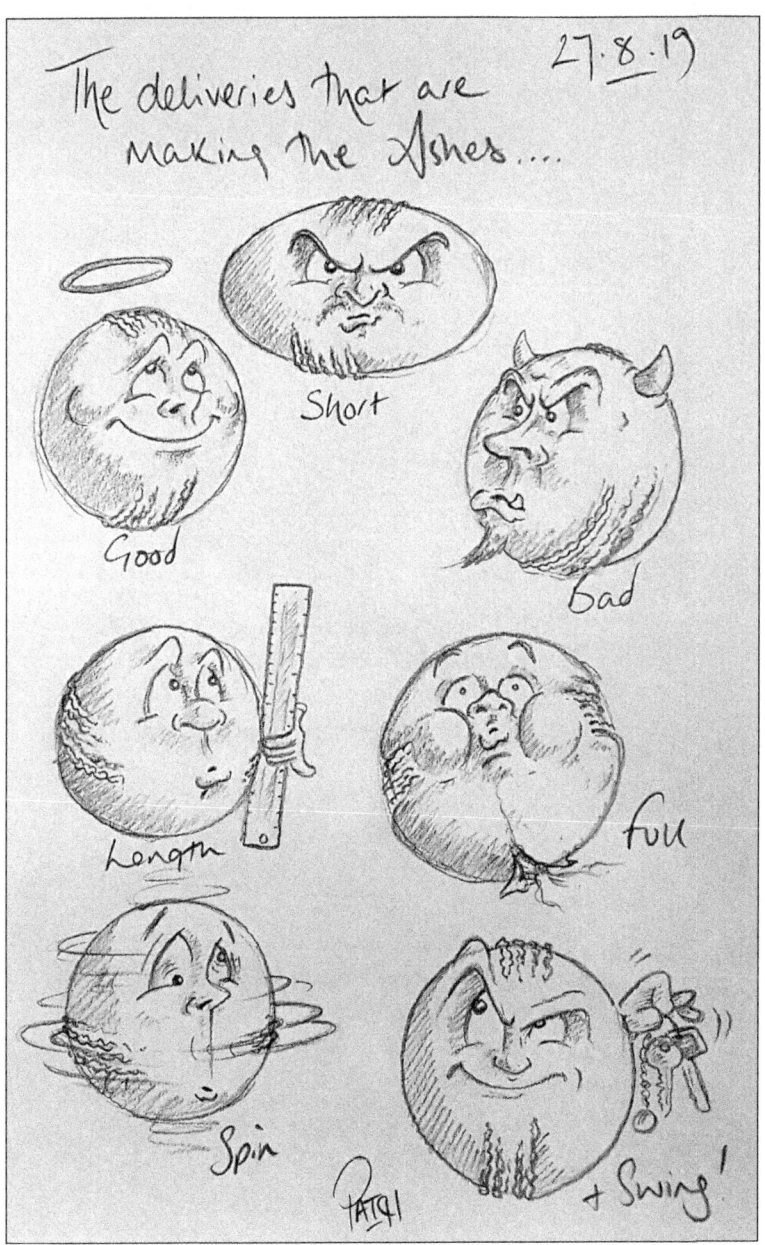

27th August 2019

What an incredible servant of
England Cricket he is..

Happy 13th anniversary Stuart!

28th August 2019

Reports coming in this morning that Nathan Lyon was helped from the field after injuring his leg in a game of Aussie Rules in the warm up to the day's play in the tour game at Derby ahead of the 4th Test..

One of these two is now fit again...

but the other...?

Who knows!

29th August 2019

Must be an Aussie turn of phrase..

Tim Paine revealed that his off spinner
Nathan Lyon is a massive weapon..
..in the upcoming test

'Locked & loaded skip...!'

30th August 2019

Mitchell Starc puts himself in contention for
a spot in the 4th Test at Old Trafford
after wickets at Derbyshire in the tour game...

..and someone finally got Steve Smith out!

31st August 2019

England consider a shake up in the order
for the 4th Test at Old Trafford
with Jason Roy dropping down to allow
Joe Denly to open...

Seems a better set up..?

Mr Langer realises that Burglar Ben and
Limpet Leach have made off with the loot...

Meanwhile, Steve Waugh makes a much
anticipated return to the Aussie camp...

2nd September 2019

In the absence of Jimmy Anderson,
Stuart Broad is joined by Craig Overton
for the 4th Ashes Test at Old Trafford
and is relishing the thought of watching
the Jofra Archer v Steve Smith showdown
from his perch at mid on!

3rd September 2019

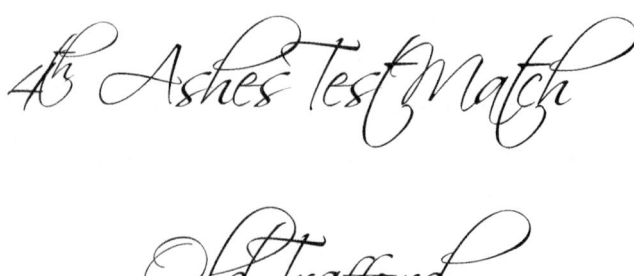

4th Ashes Test Match

-Old Trafford-

Day 1

"We've all warned Marnus about his
bubblegum nonsense on windy days before...

it was only a matter of time
before this happened..."

Close: Australia 170/3

4th September 2019

Day 2

Steve Smith puts together an incredible
double hundred to move Australia a
big step closer to retaining the Ashes.

An unfortunate no-ball from Jack Leach when
deceived Smith with a slower one and had him
caught by Stokes at slip on 118.

However good he is, though,
'The Steve' will never sound quite like..

'The Don'!

Close: Australia 497/8 dec (Smith 211), England 23/1

Day 3

Inflatables, bust boxes
and Flintoff's application...

The 'Party Stand' will never let
Nathan Lyon forget 'that drop'
at Headingley...

Close: England 200/5

6th September 2019

Day 4

Another proper day of Test cricket in Manchester, leaving the game poised nicely for more England heroics tomorrow..

Aggers absolutely on point with the euphemistic commentary today..

He stole the show with the bouncing melons line!

Close: Australia 186/6, England 18/2

Australia need 8 wickets tomorrow to retain the Ashes..

Day 5

What a fight by England to almost see out
the entire day to draw the test..

So near and yet so far.

Congratulations to Australia, unforgiving and
unrelenting with the ball today, who
retain the Ashes with The Oval Test
still to come.

Close: England 197/ao

Australia win by 185 and retain the Ashes

England 1 | Australia 2

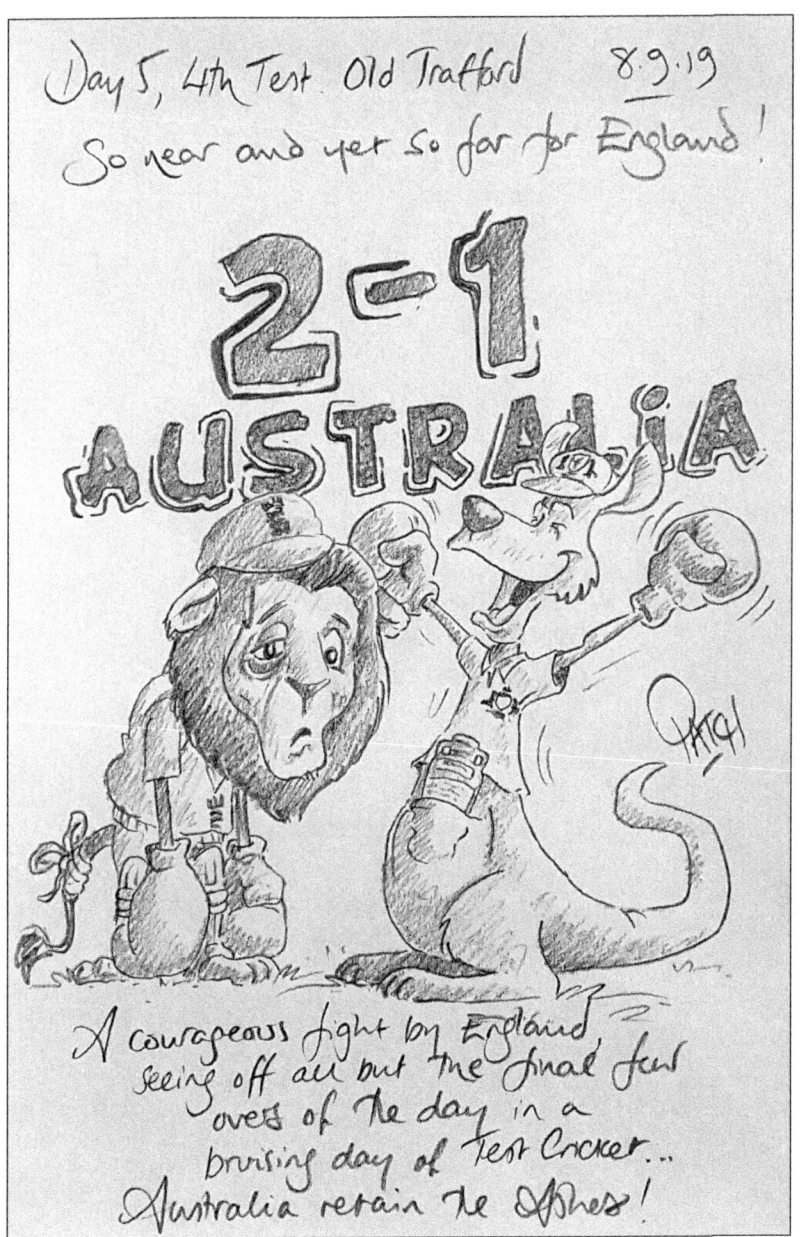

With The Ashes retained by Australia,
Colin Graves is left to break some
tricky news to Tim Paine...

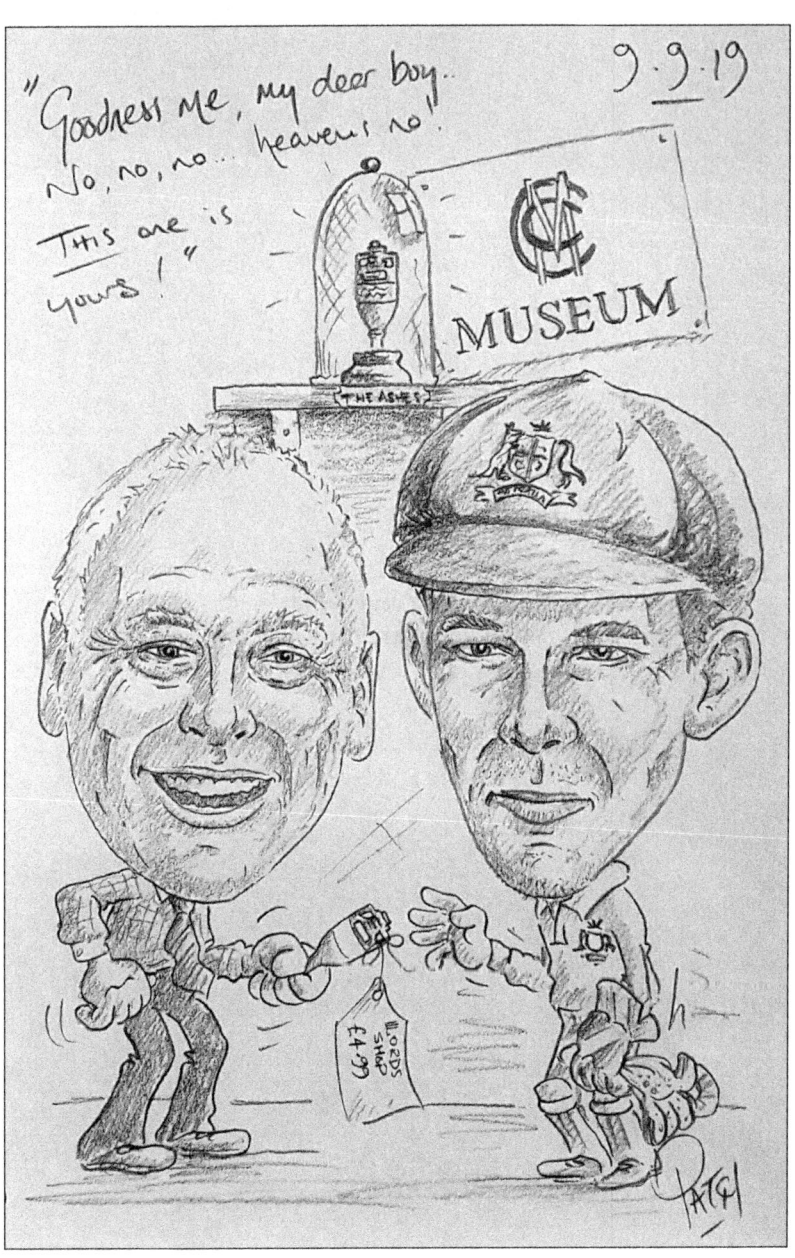

9th September 2019

Two England Ashes legends were
recognised in outgoing Prime Minister May's
honours list today..

Geoffrey had had his suit of armour
polished and ready and waiting for years...

10th September 2019

On the eve of the 5th Test at The Kia Oval,
Matthew Wade and David Warner
start strapping themselves up for one last hurrah...

11th September 2019

5th Ashes Test Match

-The Oval-

Day 1

Tim Paine asks England to bat...

Another wicket from a no-ball in the series...
Pat Cummins comes up with the solution...

Close: England 271/8 (Buttler 64*)

12th September 2019

Day 2

What a day for England..

Wickets for Jofra Archer, and England
head into day 3 with a healthy lead
and 10 wickets in hand.

Meanwhile, Tuffers takes to the TMS
drawing board to illustrate his theory
on getting Smith out...

Close: England 294/ao (Buttler 70), Australia 55/2

Day 3

Another great day for England with
Joe Denly getting so close to 100
and surely guaranteeing himself
a place on the winter tour..

Plenty runs ahead, two days to go..
but it's not over until the fat lady sings...

Warner is worryingly due runs...

Close: Australia 225/ao (Smith 80, Archer 6/62),
England 313/8 (Denly 94, Lyon 4/69)

Day 4

A wonderful victory by England
to level the series 2-2.

A Matthew Wade century kept Australia
in it for a while but Broad and Leach,
with some help from
the captain, saw them off.

The Australians celebrate retaining the Ashes
but where is Steve Smith...?

It's got to be his round?

Ah.. Yes.. Of course he is!

*Close: England 329/ao,
Australia 263/ao (Wade 117, Leach 4/49)*

England win by 15 runs

England 2 | Australia 2

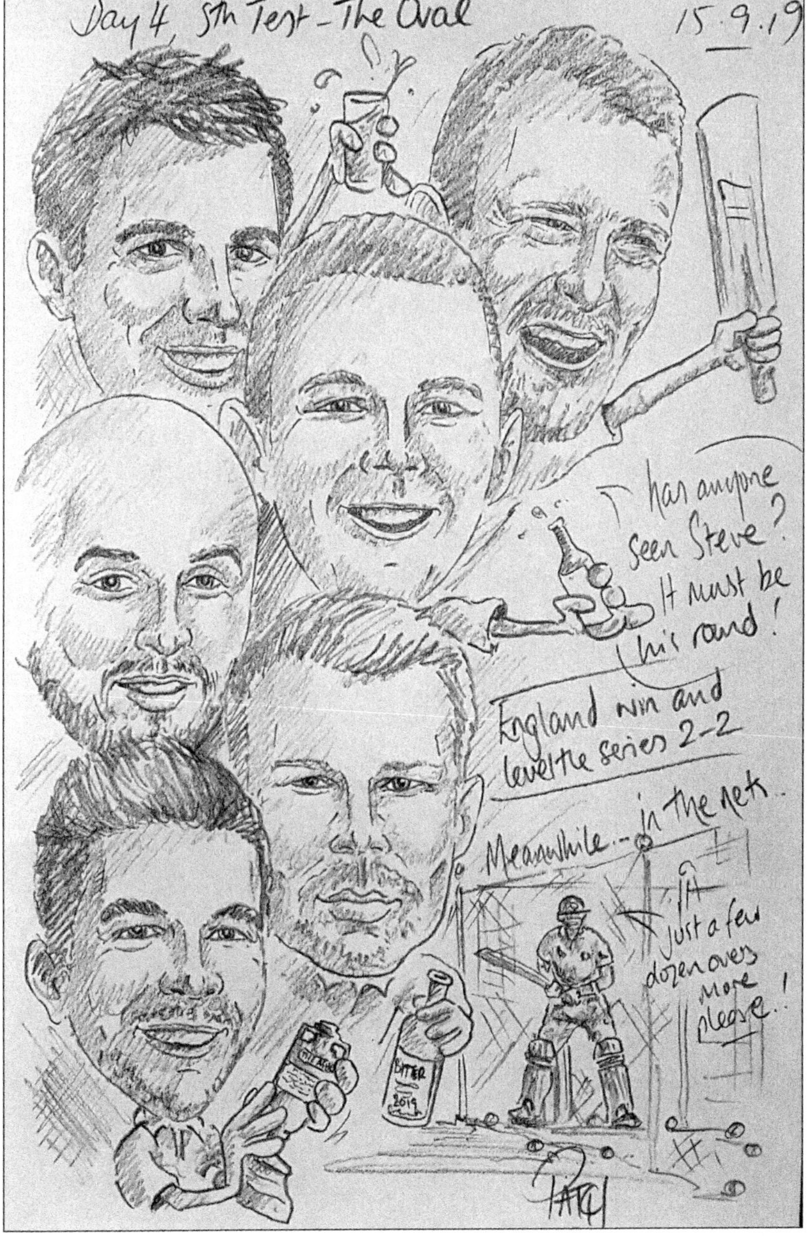

15th September 2019

The Ashes 2019 draws to a close,
and we sadly have to say some farewells..

These three have been
fantastic in their own ways.

We wish them well for the future.

Uncle Trev, Beefy & Lord G.

Thank you!

16th September 2019

#ashesillustrated

ALEADINGEDGE

A Leading Edge produces inspiring and
thought provoking cricket publications.

Patrick Latham and Wesley Durston are ex-county
cricketers, currently coaching cricket in
schools and MCCU/KSL teams respectively.

To find out more about A Leading Edge, please visit

www.aleadingedge.co.uk

or follow us on

Twitter (@aleadingedge1)

& Instagram (@aleadingedge)

#aLeadingEdge

Search for 'A Leading Edge' on Amazon
to see other books by these authors.

- A Leading Edge for Captains

Printed in Great Britain
by Amazon

38829282R00066